EARTH'S EYE

Earth's Eye
by George Keithley

STORY LINE PRESS
1994

This publication was made possible thanks in part to the generous support of the Nicholas Roerich Museum, the Andrew W. Mellon Foundation, the National Endowment for the Arts, and our individual contributors.

Book design by Lysa McDowell
Published by Story Line Press, Inc., Three Oaks Farm in Brownsville, OR 97327

ACKNOWLEDGEMENTS:
Thanks to the editors of publications in which these poems have appeared: *The Antioch Review*: "Waiting for Winter"; *Berkeley Poetry Review*: "By the Orchard Road"; *Blue Unicorn*: "The Pleading Child"; *Choice*: "It is the Dead of Winter," "The Thief's Niece," "To Bring Spring," and "When We Wake Up"; *Chowder Review*: "Girl with Green Eyes"; *Christmas Supplement* (Poetry Book Society, London): "The Quarrel"; *Corona*: "Drinking Beer in a Boat;" *The Critic*: "Visitors"; *Denver Quarterly*: "A World Apart"; *Elkhorn Review*: "Child Falling Asleep"; *Ellipsis...*: "Frightening"; *Fragments*: "Father Tein & the Swan"; *The Galley Sail Review*: "At Julia's House"; *Images*: "The Fourth Day of the Flood"; *The Iowa Review*: "The Brooding Child" and "These Small Songs"; *The Literary Review*: "Blizzard," "The Bridge," "Spoor," "Spring Snow," and "Wolf"; *Manoa*: "The Tempest Sonata"; *The Massachusetts Review*: "In Early Spring"; *New Letters*: "The Children Who Left," "Rain," and "This Field, This Lake"; *Nimrod*: "What She Knew"; *The North American Review*: "In the Sanitarium of the Sacred Heart"; *Off the Record*: "Summer, Fall, Winter, Spring" and "Supper"; *Poetry Northwest*: "In the Eternal Present All Things Are"; *Poetry Now*: "Concert Cancelled by Cold Spell," "Love May Be Glad," "Owl Has Closed His Eyes," and "Repairing the Road"; *The Poetry Review*: "The Messengers of God May Be This Busy" and "Wild Flowers"; *Pulpsmith*: "The Crime of Handel Grahm" and "Give Voice"; *The Reaper*: "Silver"; *The Seattle Review*: "The Boat"; *Song*: "Last Supper" and "Spring Is The Smallest Thing We Know"; *Spectrum*: "Gerhardt Grahm at Thirteen"; *Sponsa Regis*: "Father Tein at Five O'Clock"; *Statements*: "A Ballad for the Bride"; *Three Rivers Poetry Journal*: "If April"; *Uzzano*: "How Her Spirit Rises & Returns"; *Writer's Forum*: "The River's Sister"; and *Yankee*: "Earth Gives" and "May Morning."

"Rain" and "Wild Flowers" are included in the *Anthology of Magazine Verse and Yearbook of American Poetry*, Monitor Books; "The Boat," "The Brooding Child," "The Thief's Niece," "To Bring Spring," and "Waiting for Winter" are included in *19 New American Poets of the Golden Gate*, Harcourt Brace Jovanovich. "Girl with Green Eyes" and "Love May Be Glad" have been reprinted in *Digging In*; "The Quarrel" was reprinted in *Poetry Now*; and "Supper" was reprinted in the *Light Year* anthology, Bits Press. Thanks also to the New England Poetry Club for the Rosalie Boyle Award, for "This Field, This Lake."

The title "The Tempest Sonata" is borrowed from Beethoven's Sonata #17. I've borrowed the titles "Child Falling Asleep," "Frightening," and "The Pleading Child" from Robert Schumann's composition for piano, *Kinderszenen*.

                                                                          G.K.

For Carol

"A lake is the landscape's most beautiful and expressive feature. It is earth's eye, looking into which the beholder measures the depths of his own nature..."

Henry Thoreau,
Walden

CONTENTS

The Dead

The Seasons

EPILOGUE

PROLOGUE

IS TIME PASSING?

1. *The Crime of Handel Grahm*

Yes, I know what I did. Should I be sorry?
Yes, I was treasurer of the Grange.
Yes, I took money
from the growers: My crowbar broke
both locks off the strongbox.
There, where the office fronts the lobby,
the desk clerk stopped me.
                                    I fired once
to turn him back. A second blast, yes,
into the air. A third. To scare
the others. Now, though all was lost,
the woman lingered, her red hat framed her hair.
Over her eyes fell a delicate veil.

In jail I learned she fled on the night
train to Chicago. Many said my sin
was selfish pleasure. Lust. No. Love
of life led me to desire her.
Read the *Rock Lake Register*:
"Handel Grahm Hanged for Theft." No,
I know the life I've lived and I'm not sorry—

2. *Last Supper*

After the press and the priest depart
Julia elects to keep me company:
I sit in my cell drinking black coffee
alone with my niece. A thoughtful child
who has brought me a fresh blue shirt—

Boys from the Grange arrive with pork
roast. Red potatoes. Greens. Cold beer
and bold oaths. Eyes bright with fear,
the anxious girl shares my meal.
The jailor removes the steel knife and fork—

Like two young lawyers we eat
swiftly, licking our fingers. Soon
we part, Julia slips outdoors to join
the brash farm boys. Later I hear
the priest unlatch the gate to the street—

The jailor leads a gelding from its stall.
One guard fits its blinders on. One guard
rides before me. In the dark courtyard
he abandons the quiet priest to beat
the girl and the cursing crowd to the wall.

3. *Summer, Fall, Winter, Spring*

Jays yammer in my ears. By night a grim owl
plucks the threads of my clothes.
Gnats nest in my hair. What's left?
This flesh the rain shrivels—
It's nothing now: I shed my skin
like the snake that loves its new green shine.
When even these bones are gone,
cut down and locked with their shadow
into the loam that feeds the grass,
I give my heart to the child who sees
my eyes in the face of the moon
among the boughs—
                            All day the wind
plows its furrows across Rock Lake.
At dusk the town kneels by the brim
of the water, tells its name, and drinks
its life down to the deep stones:

Summer, Fall, Winter, Spring

4. *Give Voice*

Is time passing? Let it pass. Time is silent.
Only our souls give voice
to the years that join us. Mine with yours.
Then let them hum or talk or sing,

I want to hear what happens in this world
that lent me life. I hand it back to the elms.
To the cornstalks with their roots clamped in dark
    earth.
To the veering wind. This wind-blown world

where a man feels in his eyes the fire
from the fragrance of a woman's hair—

I want to learn if the elm stands black
and gold in the rain
and the flame of the fox burns in the brush—

To see the wolf emerge from the winter woods,
the pack like low smoke floating
on the rim of the prairie—

To know again a night of desire
more holy than the hush of the fields—

To hear our own breath tell our story—
Not the silence of the hewn stone:

> Here Lies Handel Grahm
> In Jesus' Name
> Forgiven His Sin
> & Free of His Shame

Forget that I lived, forget that I sinned.
But listen
to the thunder and the spring wind—

Earth hears the iron chime
of the courthouse clock, striking through the storm.
Across the park the tall bells
of St. Paul's reply.

The rain blows by—
Awake in its loft an owl
flaps from the barn to the waiting tree.

By the last light of day
on the wet roadbed
the crow as it claws the red meat
of the chipmunk cries *joy! joy!*

The bells, the owl, the crow, all call:
They call us tonight to come down
the road sleek from the rain
when the town lies still as the lake,
to listen as men and women
and children amazed by the pain
and delight of their lives begin to speak—

FAMILY PORTRAIT

THE THIEF'S NIECE

While the women sliced brown bread and cold meat
the thief's niece unrolled a winding sheet.
Old men leaned at the wall to count
how many masked guards the growers
hired for the ride. She walked out so hers
was the first face he might see from his mount
now it came groping into the black street.

Between two guards the council-treasurer
whispered to the priest to comfort her.
She heard the horses climbing through the dark.
The girl said there were no growers to be found—
"They have their money back." On high ground
one guard reined in his horse to mark
a limb's width. The old men haunched where they were.

The guard riding out front held the pistol
her uncle had fired—shot up the hotel
lobby, wounding a clerk. He roped the limb—
"Pray!" the girl begged. "Pray he may live!"
The priest explained, "Mercy is relative...
Yes, we'll pray now." The coroner behind him
bowed his head. Then the elders from the council.

The wives and girl sat by the tree. Nearby
the guards and jailor on horse watched the sky.
At dawn the first guard cut the councilman's
horse with a belt. It bolted and he hung
while they rode downhill. Then his friends among
the growers' younger sons and the farmhands
drew down upon his heels to help him die.

CHILD FALLING ASLEEP

1

My father's name is August,
my uncle was a thief
roped from a thick tree.
My soul shook with grief,

cold as the clear water
of Rock Lake: A quavering thing.
Still I wouldn't turn
away. I saw him fling

his long legs, swimming
in the green air and only
my brother heard me weep.
His arms could not console me—

I saw the fierce man hanging
silent among the boughs
like the moon in early morning
that pales before it falls.

2

She followed her mother through the prairie
to visit the grave—a patch of rich loam
unplanted. She shivered like the leaves
above the stones. The priest said, "Hurry,
Elke, take your daughter home—
And watch for spells. That girl's all nerves."

The porch of the white house faced the road.
Dusk blew down around the farm's
few pens. The orchard. The swirling yard.
Outside her bedroom a great elm rolled
in the wind. She ran. Ran. Both arms
out. Her hands clutched coarse bark—

3

*Shinnied up the elm
to reach that rough limb
where I once saw my lover
shining. Neither
ashamed. O, if ever
I marry, Father,
I'll be proud as any
bride in the cemetery—*

"Come down, come down!
You'll crack your crown,
you pretty child,"
Father, pleading, called
to me. Did he?
Father called me pretty?

When I do wed,
I'll bring to my bed
that thief who steals
the dark from the sky.
Hides in deep wells,
low clouds. Whose eye
in the dead of winter
is the blaze of ice on the river.

4

"A sweet success!" crows the groom.
Julia Grahm has married the moon—
Badger, browser, don't spoil their sleep
tonight. Will you watch where you step!

Quiet owl! They're barely awake.
Corn rows and thistles whisper. Look—
Her eyes half-close. Gladly she stirs
in his lustrous arms, his gaze on hers

until its glow dims in her mind.
The moon is down. Under the wind
they lie alone in the cool fields—
The dark chamber of the deep weeds.

5

Almost asleep tonight in her bed
she finds starlight in the high trees. Hears
the last of her prayers: "If you bless
this world come down and sing the dead
to life." Her room falls still. Now the stars
enter floating, flaming, singing *yes*.

RAIN

August watches from the porch, one hand
spread upon the screen like a star.
No stars. Lightning flares. He hears
both his hounds prowling around the pond.
Thunder disturbs the brim
where his wife's chrysanthemums
color the water with their blooms:
Red rust, egg yolk, white plaster.

Every blossom is a gaudy crown
unwilling to bow
to the ground
in the gravity of rain.

The odor of a dark storm
swarms
in her hair, unribboned,
tumbling down her lilac gown.
In bed they listen to the rain
rattle the whole house now.
Roof, walls, porch, pasture.
All the earth saturated, shaken, still—

How long her hair is
rolling over his shoulder.
This is what he will remember after
forgetting her flowers. (There in the rain

they bow.)

WOLF

He heard the wolf running.

He was ten, he lay in the dark, listening. Heard it racing around the corners of the house, snapping and yelping.

Then the wolf stole out beyond the woods quiet as ice.

Once it found its feet in the open prairie nothing could touch it. It laid its ears back and bolted over the frozen fields. It startled their old privy that screeched like an owl. He heard the barn groan, his house clenched its teeth against each gust. Outside his window the pale wolf bristled.

It roamed everywhere in the night, shaking itself, howling.

Later he knew it had leaped down to the lake. The wind crept lower, circling the ice.

The next day he sat on the wooden sled, the hatchet in his lap. He watched his father fish the black hole they had chopped almost round; a dark eye staring into the ice.

Motor oil stained his father's gloves, fish oil had softened them. Old leather like a second skin, more comfortable than cotton. His dark fingers worked a line so thin the boy's eyes lost it when he blinked. He rubbed his eyes dry and looked across the ice.

The boy saw the wolf lope out of the woods, white as though it wore the snow. Romping there, rolling over. Now it rose up glistening, frothing. The man watched the hole in the ice go grey as the sky rolled over and he whispered, "Snow."

WILD FLOWERS

Whenever I bring her flowers she cries.
Best of all I like to pick
white daisies growing wild
there in the hayfield. Or I find,
bright in one untrampled corner,
their slim silken stems intact,
a few delicate bluebells. Moist
clusters the color of her eyes.
I remember my mother at some moment
of every daylight hour. Only
in my sleep I might forget her.
Why does she never come to meet me?

By the fence, on my knees to fetch
her gift. And not to slip away.
Never will I leave her. Never
return to school, the taunting boys
grinning. Games. Cunning or clever
tricks. Other girls quick
to laugh. Lunge. Blood in my mouth
tastes like dirt but bitter. This grass
is home. Quiet behind the storm
fence, here I'll stay. In plain view
of our house, I kneel and gather
a fistful of timorous blue blossoms.

I want to hear her laugh at this
little bouquet. Before the glassy weather
breaks. But the grass shivers
under my hands—I start up—
Sudden thunder. Loud. Like horses
that pour across our poor fence
into the pasture in first flower.
Huge horses unbridled, black as trees
when a storm shakes its wet hair
over their limbs. Routed by the rain,
I run through the trembling grass—
I cry out, I cry out for my mother.

THE PLEADING CHILD

After Christmas Mass the strains
of carols call us to the flesh
and blood figures in the stable créche:
"Joy to the world! the Savior reigns..."
Joseph, Mary, and the Child in white.
Kneeling, the Kings set down their pomp
and gifts. We troop into the night—
Moon, lift up your little lamp.

The stone bridge straddles the stiff creek.
Skate blades slung back, two sharp boys slip
off the ice. Beyond the bridge we grip
each other's hands to climb the bleak
hill. My sister whispers, "Look!"
Fresh tracks pock the snow, dogs romp
down the road in a ragged pack—
Moon, lift up your little lamp.

Something more than the snow or chill
makes my mother stop and weep.
Something her heart has hidden deep
within the winter pulses still:
Silent in the sparkling dark,
lovers bundle past the pump
house and pause. Only their eyes speak—
Moon, lift up your little lamp.

Father shoulders Julia over
a steep drift. Why do I cry?
Mother's singing, "...the sounding joy,
Repeat the sounding joy." I shiver
in my short coat and she stoops to fold
her arms around me. Gladly we tramp
home across the glittering cold—
Moon, hold up your happy lamp!

FRIGHTENING

If we love God we have nothing to fear, says the priest. "Fear not, little flock," he reads from *Saint Luke*. God sends our guardian angels to keep us from harm. They're not like men or women, he says, they never marry... I glance at my mother and father listening. I watch my sister Julia playing with her purse.

Do our angels grow old? I don't know. But I'm sure they die. I think they die before they arrive. My uncle Handel stole money from the onion growers. One night men took him from the jail. When they hanged him, did they kill his angel too? Or his angel wasn't there.

Here in Rock Lake we're a long ride by train from Chicago. Mother says it's a difficult trip; when we go to the city we pack sandwiches and bring pillows. Mostly we stay home. All winter. It's often dark and it snows. I don't ask how our angels can find us here. I don't ask how they can travel so far. But remember, they never eat, and they can't keep each other warm. They leave Heaven hoping to help every soul on earth. But it's a dark, cold journey and few survive. If any.

Father Tein doesn't tell us how the angels come to Rock Lake. He closes the doors of the tabernacle. Silently we walk to the rail to receive communion. In his large hand the pale wafer trembles. With eyes down we walk back to our pews. It isn't *right*. I know it isn't... My sister's older, and my parents and the priest know better. But I know it isn't right. If God is in this bread it should taste like bread. The best bread ever—crisp and full and warm and sweet. But it doesn't. It lies dry on my tongue. It sticks to the roof of my mouth and it tastes like nothing at all. I nudge it with my tongue. Little by little it loosens, it dissolves. Soon I've swallowed it. God is in me now. But that tasteless bread is gone. God is here and gone. It isn't *right*. But everyone is kneeling among the pews. The church is so quiet I hear my father's watch ticking. How old is he? His hair is thick but going grey. Like little ashes there. Then I hear someone walking up the aisle... I look around. The woman moves with a nervous grace like my mother. In the folds of her long green robe there are dark shadows. Wet shadows like the pools of mud and rainwater that stand all summer in the woods.

Does Julia see her? No, my sister's head is bowed in prayer, her brown hair covers the shoulders of her blue dress. Her eyes are closed over her missal as if she's asleep. I look back at the woman approaching. Her face is serious, her eyes are kind and sad. She stops at our pew to touch my arm.

She takes my hand; I rise and we walk toward the altar together. The priest and the altar boys move aside. I've never stepped beyond the communion rail—and here I stand in front of the tabernacle that houses the Host! I tell myself this should be frightening. But it isn't, the terror comes later.

Before us now the doors of the little tabernacle loom up to overshadow the altar itself. They've grown huge, like the doors of the barn behind our house. They open for her and we walk into the loft... I look down at the straw-covered floor. Many families have left the Mass to crowd in and kneel among the cows. The cows stand silent... the grownups are busy at their prayers. They work their rosaries, the beads drop through their fingers in slim lines like flies walking down the flanks of the cows. I turn to ask the woman why we're here: Is this God's secret place?

"Yes. And you must speak softly."

"Why?"

"Because we're in church," she says.

We lie down in the hay. I'm happy and I don't know why, maybe it's because she said we're in church and here we are in the barn. I begin to laugh. We lie in the hay, laughing. But Father Tein must think I'm lost. Clutching his robes around his knees, he rushes into the barn. He searches every corner for me, he says I'm a lost soul. His altar boys carry candles up the ladder. They stumble into the loft and the candles fall. The hay catches fire; a roaring heat surrounds me. In the roar I hear the woman weeping. I search wildly. But she's nowhere to be seen in the burning air. I try to climb free of the flames but I'm falling. It isn't right! I wasn't lost, I was happy here... I know this now, I'll never live as long as my father. Falling to my death, I'll burst into light like the angels. God sends them to guard us but they never arrive. They're torn apart by the terrible journey; shreds of their bright wings drift down all winter. I run from the barn to the house. The cold air burns my face. My sister's too. The snowfall, she says, is beautiful. But it's already gone, I tell her. I've caught the snow on my tongue and it tastes like nothing at all. I've caught it in my hands and they're empty and cold. No one comes to help us here. No one keeps us from harm. She holds me in her arms, she can't see why I'm shouting and crying. "It isn't right," I tell her, "I *know* it isn't."

THE BROODING CHILD

In my dream the brooding child
I was ten years ago leans far
back, tilting his kitchen chair,
to hear the Chicago Symphony
of the Air. No one else is home
until the strings and horns fall still.
A sudden crowd swarms the room—
Grey-eyed uncles and aunts, and Father
and Mother. My sister Julia, too.
It might be every holiday reunion.
If I were younger I would guess
my First Communion. It's not,
though someone has invited Father Tein,
who thought he was a friend of mine.

Their faces are flames that glow
without the weight of guilt.
Their voices know my name—
"Gerhardt!" they cry. Or simply
"Gary!" if it's my sister. Always
I look as if I'm listening.
Now they command my attention
their mouths form an important shape—

"You can be anyone you want.
Anyone at all!"

        I smile.
They blaze into ordinary air.
Why should they stay? I recall
their message vividly. They dare
not fester in restless sleep
like some hallucination out of Hell.
Mostly they're my family, you see.

And because I was taught every dream
is a delusion, telling you this
just now I smiled. Still
in the dream I understand they mean
what they say: "Be anyone at all"

but not that child.

THE TEMPEST SONATA

A grey day in April—
Thunder fills the wells to the brim.
Tall elms tremble.
We walk the orchard road to the grave of my uncle.

Our parents hurry us home, the storm
swells in the wind—
Over the turned earth
it sets the fields on fire,
flashing bright and black.

     Let my body break
     its solitude
     and speak in
     song, in spirit
     with the throbbing air.

I trudge into my mother's study.
The piano is enormous furniture.
The art of playing is to make it disappear—

Why do we say
we play music? It isn't play,
this melody I make for my sister—

I want her music to fly free of my body
unable to bear the stern stillness
before the first note
like the low sky before rain—

I want her not to see
the boy beating on the keys, weeping
with wild, delicious dread—

Afraid of the beauty within
men and women, how could I know
we are ourselves piano, woodwind, horn?

Too late we learn the throat is the magic flute—
With every breath our dying words are sung.

GERHARDT GRAHM AT THIRTEEN

Behind a taut cotton curtain   pale as its purity
which quakes with each breath   of the boy kneeling
silent in his own darkness,   secluded in the antique
sweltering confessional,   the priest speaks of puberty.

His silhouette looms upon   the gauze. This profile
of the priest is a shadow   cast upon the thin fabric
of his words, his voice   unwavering, the only light
admitted to the mute booth   where the blond boy burns.

"Father, forgive me, but   I wonder, do you ever feel
there's nowhere to hide?   And you can't help it. You
want to run. Run away."   No reply. His fists open.
Out from the church he rushes   into the narrow street.

His sister Julia, sprawled   laughing on a sprung sofa
banished to the breezeway,   rolls a pink plum stone
on her oval lips, half-teasing.   Sucking, swallowing.
"It's sex, Gary, you're young.   Why do you worry so?"

Does no one hear this cry?   No, he won't ask her.
All the world is his witness,   call it what they will:
Still its wings stroke   the bleeding light, relentless
it roams Rock Lake, circling,   like a hungry hawk.

A WORLD APART

Julia's brother wrote
his final song for her
before his plane was lost
over Africa, in the war.

Time and again she sang—
Her friends, her family
listened long in the shade.
Starlings flocked to the tree.

She taught us Africa meant
mad elephants, dry air
on fire. The grasses lean
and brown, the mudholes bare.

Birds of brilliant plumage
shrieking: *Planes that roar*
out of the dawn to strafe
the tents on the burning floor.

They shell the tanks. Oil drums
ignite. Two planes attack
the water trucks and vanish
in a black burst of flak—

Skoronsky the young scholar
argued, "No analogy
ever should be drawn
from war's brutality."

But Julia disagreed:
"In this world every soul
knows the pain of birth—
The great beast or the small

child or whistling bird.
Each life is strange and frail
and suffers its sudden death,
human and animal."

"Clearly," Skoronsky scoffed,
"a culture ruled like ours
by rational thought and will
is a world apart from theirs."

And he left her by the starlings
that trilled their reckless tune
while elephants came walking
through the brittle afternoon.

WHAT SHE KNEW

Nearer to dream than daylight when she heard it,
still she slept. Until she willed herself awake.
So suddenly the initial silence fell, it shattered
the sensible music in Julia's mind. She
pressed her palms upon her eyes. Kept them there.
So she forbid light to uncurtain the day
and disrupt what she knew was no dream:
promise of a dark summer rain.
She lay in bed waiting for the water to rise,
to draw her dry elbows down, to drench her flesh,
pale as bone. Lifting slim legs, arms akimbo,
she felt the flood swell up until it swept her
soundlessly downstairs, out the storm-torn door,
gliding under the correct clock on City Hall,
the drowned town awash beneath her. No one to grasp her
trailing hand, a rudder unhinged in the current.
No one to plead for her to stay. Or insist
she put up her hair in that netted bun, pack
her midnight blue dress, her other shoes, and climb
into the rasping white van to return
to the county home. No one to kiss *goodbye*
before her corpse (if this were death;
she did not think it was, so soon) should drift, rising
and falling, the least of burdens, downriver in the swift rain.

Let them search for her when the water sinks
into the peat bog and the sodden sacred acres
of their hoped-for Heaven. Lucid, alert,
still she lies in the dark her hands hold down
and it will be awhile before they miss her;
busy with that other nuisance now. The rain.
She hears its warm whisper: *Stay with us.*
Clapping shutters. Streaming eaves. Then
the hush as every squirrel, cock, and hen,
every cat in the county is driven to cover
under the dripping syllables of the rain: *Stay
with us, this will pass, this will soon blow over.*

THE LOVERS

IF APRIL

If April is to green the earth again
Rock Lake will unlock with shuddering sighs
when love lies down with death in the dark rain

easing the ice, so the slow floes drain
into the swelling stream. We'll hear it rise,
if April is to green the earth again

where the willows stir, shaking that satin sheen
from their stiff skirts, the fine snow from our eyes.
Though love lies deep with death in the dark rain

rumpling their bed, on the blue mud we've seen
the first loon wade, or waddle, before he flies.
If April is to green the earth again

soon will that demon deep-diving loon
shatter the water with his witless cries.
Must love lie still as doom in this dark rain?

The lake's awake! We hear the hooting loon,
loud, loud, beneath our somber skies—
If April is to green the earth again,
Love, we'll lie warm and laugh in the dark rain.

MAY MORNING

On a rainy May morning, lying dead
quiet, wrapped in this weather, we hear
the wind stop. Then the irregular beat
of water strumming on the street,
draining the darkness from the air.

On a rainy May morning, shaking her hair
while her hands search out her clothes,
my bride unbends like a sweet linden tree
burdened with bloom as gradually
the storm rises and the grey room glows.

IN EARLY SPRING

1

In early spring I felt the weight
of his legs
upon my own. I undid my dress,
we watched the wind row
across the water. At once then all
my dread
began. As if my soul
grew wary, troubled by the low splash
of the lake, and the chill that gripped the
earth

where we lay beneath the curtain
of willows.
I leaped up to leave. Brushing, then, my
clinging clothes, afraid
he would force me down. Still I delayed,
I stroked
the cold light on his hair,
looking into the leaves, asking now
how will I live? What will become of me?

2

No, she told me. *No, we'll be lost!*
Fanned the fresh
wrinkles from her damp dress, fled uphill
and drove home. Her car
buzzing behind the webs of trees and
blazing
water. Waiting, I saw
a second couple nimbly climbing
down the steep hill and straying toward the shore.

I tried tracing the chains of young
leaves, restless,
eager for her. The ache like a rock
sinking in my sex.
If the face of God is ecstasy
it is
a membrane of moist light
throbbing in the willows, and I won't
save myself, I have always lived like this.

THE BRIDGE

When you are near my words are the worked stones
in the bridge over Rock River, solid syllables
lugged up from the mud, set upon each other.
Ice impacts every surface. Grey rains shine.
Boots beat them smooth, and wheels. Hooves, too.

No amount of traffic wears away
their dumb weight. They sleep like sheep
under April frost until the flicker
of your eyes in a green breeze
brushes the water, and the stones, the sheep,

go leaping into summer.

THE QUARREL

1

Our basket is shut, wax wrappings packed in it.
    Coffee and the gold cans of ale
        drunk, while we quarrel alone.

Only a mile east of the village limit
    pickups, vans, cars, transport the pale
        light into late afternoon.

We rise. Your coat. The basket. Wait one minute
    while a brisk wind troubles the trail
        those two horses amble down.

2

Green the shade, green and yellow the blowing grass
    their pasture yields, where the quick course
        of Rock Creek has carved its width

side to side, through bottomland gentle as moss.
    How we'd like to drop our remorse
        in the cool grass. Down the path

the mare loiters shy. The stallion loping past
    crops her mane, and the courted horse
        happily tramples the earth.

SPRING IS THE SMALLEST THING WE KNOW

Spring is the smallest thing we know, the least
noise we listen to is the speech of bees,
who cruise a field for clover and as they pass
whisper *science* to the tacit grass—

grass that multiplies around a man
remembering damp shadows on the land
this spring and every spring until he dies;
grass that grows like rain before our eyes.

Rain is the longest law we've ever seen;
taller than all our thoughts of trees, the rain
reduces every distance, dear, to here,
where we lie waiting for the wind to clear

a sullen sky and bring the singing wren—
this bird who stirs such music in the sun
he wakes our dim world from its winter trance,
and makes your warm legs dream and my hands dance.

THE DEAD

LOVE MAY BE GLAD

The clear eye of the lake—
Once it was the only witness
to dragonflies flitting over the water.
Her hand on his, her touch as light as theirs.

Who heard their whispers that summer evening?
The wind was up.
On a taut rope their boat nodded *yes*,
slipped its mooring and drifted into dusk.

Pretty pictures please us, until we see
where the stern struck rock.
Thrust up on shore
in winter the prow pockets snow.
The eye all ice now.

Ice too has its say. It says stay
close to cold fact
that shelters fantasy and keeps it deep
until the lake unlocks
this story in time.

A story telling us

the eye is ours
open to the blue or blank
with cold. Telling us

love may be glad and green
in a world as brief as this,
as brutal as their words were beautiful.

SILVER

Over the frozen lake the wind shines.
Over the prairie it shivers
the migrant camp: Foxes, Sioux,
Winnebagos left behind when the buses rolled
south after harvest. All night
they drift into the Dry Dock Inn. Growers, too,

and their white wives. Over the tavern road
the moon spills its blood
in the wind. Fretfully, as the glow
of scarlet candles warms
her eyes, Erica sheds
her coat of wool and snow.

The jukebox wails blues. Her husband orders
corn whiskey, clips
his tobacco. Tucks the sleek
blade in his boot. She drains her glass and roams
the dance floor. When he calls
Erica shakes her yellow hair—

He hears her laughter as the rhythms stir
her skirt. Wabashaw, a fieldhand
half Sioux, walks her way
and grins. Wicks in tin cups
fling at their feet the shadows
hawks cast on summer hay—

Shadow wings which circle
the couple as they spin
in slow time. They turn, stare.
Twice the steel gleam strikes—
Breathless in each other's arms
they cling, falling to the floor.

Two off-duty deputies handcuff
her husband, phone the coroner:
Mueller's battered Buick arrives.
The bartender obliges, helps carry
both bodies. "So damn quick—
One dance. It cost two lives!"

Mueller blows on his fingers,
fumbles for the keys.
His ancient stationwagon, broad
as a hearse, wallows toward town
like a boat too low in the water—
A black boat sinking in the road.

The wolf whose thirst has lured her
onto the lake, watches
the wagon crawl out of sight.
When her raw tongue lolls
over the ice unsatisfied,
her throat opens to the night—

The wind, pure silver, howls.

THE BOAT

1

Where is the woman who unmoored this morning,
rowing upriver to visit her sister?
Toward noon her skiff rides so high
its keel climbs free of the current.

No one to work the oars,
they drag silver ribbons like whispers
her children trail through the sedge grass.

2

Into blue shadow her boat
drifts under the arch of the stone bridge.

3

The boat brightens floating in crimson light,
more earth than air in it.

Light at the last hour
downstream where the yolk of the sun breaks,
bleeding in the water.

THE RIVER'S SISTER

Emil Mueller, M.D.:

Hunters' trucks, my black wagon, the sheriff's car,
idle now. We gather by the river,
we hear its hum and wonder
what was the pain you couldn't bear?
Reporters approach with cameras and tape—
Our somber column crawls through the fields into town.

An aging man with a wife and unwed daughter,
I have questions beyond procedure
a coroner's practice fails to answer.
The autopsy is obscure: No scars.
No bruises, contusions.
Belly not bloated. Neither
pregnant again nor long in the water.

How easily loneliness enters the soul,
as lightly as a young mother steps
into a little boat. It faintly sways
to the pull of oars as she disappears
beneath the brown willows only
to float into my helpless hands—

Sister of the river,
you are sorrow endless and young, silence
with no one to forgive.
You are what cannot be saved by our learning or love.
At the end of your journey I wait
to greet you with my dumb grief—
You are with us always but you never arrive.

VISITORS

What can we tell his widow when she's lost
poor Jack? One clear morning, blustery,
bright, he climbed that sharp roof to repair
shingles the wind worked loose. His history
fell hard from his hands: Drunk on despair
and pale as rain, she serves us tea and toast.

Once when they had planted seed, he said:
"Marlena, our own sons will work this wheat."
None came. Daughters neither. Harvest nights,
fieldhands and neighbors jostled for a seat
in her snug kitchen. Turning up the lights,
they drank his sweet wine and broke bread

baked in her oven all those Saturdays.
In town he bought the black rooster hammered
onto the barn to point which way the wind
has shifted; also feed her hens clamored
after. Arriving late, our mayor has pinned
his armband on. His aunt at the piano plays

so long Marlena contemplates her chores
and yellow callouses. One cousin names a salve
she might try. Father Tein, ill at ease,
reasons: "Brief visits are best. Love

endures even death." Together we rise,
he brushes his black hat. We step outdoors.

The priest remains to praise her husband's ferns.
"October is a torch! Look how these hang
on the air like fire—" Leaves whirl in the orchard
Jack pruned each autumn. The wind bears the tang
of black pears. It scales the roof where his misfortune
nailed fast the iron weathercock, which turns.

IN THE SANITARIUM
OF THE SACRED HEART

"I saw spirits gliding among the flames"
Purgatorio XXV

White flurries immerse
the day. March weather
darkens, dusk combs her cold hair.
Lord, how have I sinned
if Little Boy brought this peace?
Sister says, *Lie down.*

Wake to hear the robin sing
in the maple: *Spring! It's Spring!*

The breezy day-nurse
skips by, her sweater
swirling over her shoulder—
April night. That wind,
pursuing dark flocks of geese,
at dawn drops the moon.

Squirrels so red they scorch the trees
interrupt these reveries—

While a blue jay screams
in an oak the priest
brings bread. Down the winding drive
the gardener's fire
crackles and alarms the loud
bird fleeing the oak,

piercing the shade with his fear
of the flapping flames. I hear

his cry in my dreams.
These visions, Sister,
persist: 8/6/45
as we climb higher
into heaven, the black cloud
boiling. Cinders, smoke.

Hiroshima burns beneath
the blind wind, city of death

in life, the slim child
bleeding from her ears.
The blank face of her mother
broiled pink, no mouth left
to cry. They hear such shrill pleas
all doctors ignore

these silent cases: A man's eyes
melt in their sockets; horseflies

attack his flesh. Mild-
mannered, he appears
with those long dead who gather
in my sleep. I wet
my sheets and fall to my knees,
sobbing on the floor.

Maples harden. Cold nights drift
into Advent. Now the gift

of a damp snow drapes
the motor-test wing
and clinic garden. I've seen
from my window-loft
every blade of ice a knife
honed to carve my soul

from this flesh! and Nature still
dares to teach us how to heal—

At noon in blue capes,
white gloves, boots, three young
nurses slant across the lawn.
The tall girl looks lost
in thought. Then I hear her laugh,
lighter than the snow.

BY THE ORCHARD ROAD

1

By the orchard road red blossoms gleam.
The burial party lowers its box below
an arch of petals, a plum branch shedding
perfume. While they pray
he's like a colt confined to the small pasture,
the tearful man trampling the shade.
His wife is the brown-eyed girl they leave
alone by the grave. Young arms folded
beneath her bosom hold her full-grown grief.

2

Cautiously the priest's coupe follows
the funeral wagon onto the road
into town. Under the plum trees
the odor of motor oil
stains the air like smoke.
From a heart-shaped spade
the couple scrapes off loam—
The two start home, their truck
trailing its twin tread of black mud.

3

All spring the winds wash the white stone crosses.
The liquid life of the soul
crawls over water and soil—
Downhill from the orchard road
a green snake glides to the rim
of the rain pool warm
as the mouth of a well.
Around Rock Lake yellow pollen slides
alongshore, sucking at the black bank, the brilliant grasses.

THE SEASONS

IN THE ETERNAL PRESENT
ALL THINGS ARE

floating on
the Rock River, green limbs and rippling
images of limbs
dragging leaves in the quarrelsome current.
You listen to
their hissing, you
hear it as discontent,
mindful of midsummer
air, muggy, sullen; a slowly shifting sky
where you see a hawk hover, far and deep.

The hawk rows
in a warm wind across the orchard
acre crows nest in
to the elm and oak woods behind the lake.
While the rain swells
around her, she
hunches low in an oak
dry under the near limbs:
she is the jump into the wind, the brown glide
and the fall to green cover, braked and steep.

The full length
of the riverbed the rain searches
the murky water;

no rowboats, outboard motors. Just upstream
turbines turn eight
generators
3,600
rpm, spinning off
a small waterfall, the spillage coursing out
to the stone-blue lake in a silent sweep.

When the trout
sinks in dark water two fishermen
laugh, turning. They hoist
their poles up the steps of the power plant,
watching a hawk
fly the green woods
to the river. The rain
blows by. Beside a rock
the trout rides, holding under the current his
sudden lunge, the rise, the swift silver leap.

THE MESSENGERS OF GOD
MAY BE THIS BUSY

butterfly   over the iris
            fussing

    or that   yellow wings
            one warm

                snow
    or are they   white? Now

                intruder
        a black   dances

    briskly this
                way.
                        All three

            we knew
        bring news   once, woven

    of the fabric
                        old
            of heaven:

                scarves

shirts
                    the red gloves

you lost
                    to the lake
            on your way

            its bold blue
all summer   eye open.

GIRL WITH GREEN EYES

None of them knows my name
is Faye Niemeyer. *Green Eyes!*
Green Eyes! they call me.
The milktruck men laughing
beyond the barbwire fence—
Green Eyes, come with us!

I turn away. The field overflows
emerald light warm
as Rock Lake in a spring. Never talk
to strangers I was told.
What a pretty one!
Like a ride into town?

I glance back this once.
Young men with yellow hair
I see drive by every week—
none of them knows my name.
We'll learn you how to dance.
My feet hide under the fence.

On my legs I feel rising
the wind at play in the weeds
weaving the light. Strum
of long grasses when they waltz
in the wind. Sun a silk skirt!

You catch your tongue in the pump?

I can speak.

Their large hands lift me up.

Straw heaped all around
tall iron cans
that sweat like stones in the cold
truck lurching down the road.

SUPPER

Twitching, sniffs the liverwurst
sandwich left too long in this
crinkled lunchbag. Suppose she
noses into it? Mouse can't
help rattling walls thin as her
luck. Footsteps? Stops; ears quiver.
Fast feast. Pacing the paper
floor, she eats. Eats and paces,
panting. Burrs of onion bread
cling to her whiskers. Licks, licks
paws *(pause)*. Claws click. Little time
to escape, squeezing, belly-
low, under the thumb-width warp
of the kitchen door. To creep
through the twilight trembling, full
of fright. Across warm grass no
shadow floats, falls. O lovely
summer supper! Owl's asleep.

DRINKING BEER IN A BOAT

You forget you left an oar loose. You forget
the hour. A duck sees the sun set—
Dives after it. He retrieves
a spark in each eye. I lie
drinking beer in a boat
and hear these dipsy little dirges.
Is someone humming under the gunnels?
I sit up, afloat on the moon. (No
trick. Look. I walk over the chalk-
white brow.) Down. Dark. Floundering
free of the boat, what strikes me
is that stray oar. Swim for it. Or
poor Peter's a joke in the morning paper:
    "Plumber Drowns in Rock Lake"
Dead in the water. Listen, why
should any plumber be a swimmer?
If we're worth a damn we're high and dry.
(Keep it up, Peter!) Toes touch stones.
Wade through ink to shore, tumble over
the other oar. Onto rock. Bruised
blue, soaked to the teeth, not quite dead
of fright. For what welcome? You
mock me all the while. But who?
Who in Hell would roost in the night
and hoot at my misfortune? *Who,*

indeed. Owl, was that a smile?

REPAIRING THE ROAD

1

Summer sunning itself on the broken road—
This river of heat
floats in the air and dissolves at our feet.

Six men sent to repair
split concrete
work without a word:

Two scatter sand
behind the tar tank, its black belly
sweetly steaming.

But two of us tired of working
with the weasel in our crew
ease up, seeing him slip
his whiskey to the foreman's son.

Dropping our pails we cross a field
flush in milkweed, white fur
puffed out. When the pod unpeels,
its seeds like souls of the dead
free of their flesh
fly across the gravel bed
of the Northwestern rails. Here,

walking above the blue thistle-burr
and thatchwork vines
we reach town in good time—
Sundown leaves light enough to swim.

2

The priest locks the doors of St. Paul's.
Girls gather on the stairs
of the green bandstand, two police
patrol the park, in low gear
three cars prowl the street.
The trees turn darker than the hour.

3

The scent of imminent rain
weighs on the air, on the water
heavy as desire.
Lightning flares, falls
over Rock Lake like a net—
We sink in each other's arms

only to rise, swimming for shore.
The girls dress quickly, wet
palms primming their hair.
Headlights search
the scarred arm of the road

scrubbed by rain. Night clears—

The Hunter and his Dog enter the park
between forbidding spires on the sky:
a severe steeple over City Hall
opposite the stark steel cross of St. Paul—
Images the eye
forms in the dark where our hopes lie.

THIS FIELD, THIS LAKE

Over Rock Lake, this morning, all morning
the sun levitates like a lucky kite.
At noon we untie it from the pier.
Birds row their voices across the day.

How can the place of our birth be wrong?
Born in blood, we know the near
tide pulse, or pull. Its surge and sway
until the rag-tailed sun takes flight.

Though all birds follow and disappear
behind the sky, our souls at play
plead: O let us live day and night
blazing in the body where we belong—

This field of flesh, this lake of light
about us is our being, but we hear
dark music in the mind and steal away
deep into night where we sing, we sing.

FATHER TEIN & THE SWAN

Why do I find no peace in this place? Impatient
with our null autumn weather
in which the last pheasants nest. Hunters steal
behind our rectory half-hidden by the wild
berry bushes neither tall nor thick enough to conceal
their rusting pickup beside the road.
Prowling the field, hounds flush a hen
from her cover, vines tangled
over the drainage ditch. Two shots
and they fetch her. They flush another, drop her.
The men, returning, leap the low culvert,
start toward town and the oncoming dark. Both dogs
too skittish to sit, strutting in the bed of the truck.

Two men, their dogs, the dead birds, vanish
down that chill road into November night.
Night whose silence kneels in me.
Toolshed, henhouse, stables.
Across the pasture I walk out
through the thatch of brush, thistles, weeds, the prairie
white as Rock Lake in winter,
now the wind has raised the moon
like a swan gliding from the grass.
Jesus, too, haunts our childhood when we believe
he rises, strewing light. Tonight will I hear
those bright wings beat for love? For love?

SPOOR

The odor is in the place, not the pellet.
Try to ignore it
as you unwrap these brown oblong bundles.

Forget, if you can, the leaves bloodied underfoot.
Forget this scent that stains the leathery leaves.
Like fire in the dry grass it smokes out
red November rising behind your eyes.
You blink it back to see
the innards are missing.
Not one thread of muscle remains.
Notice too the needle-fine unraveled spine.
No surprise the shoulders
appear so straight when they wear no meat.

Recall how the low forelegs
depend upon these claws, picked clean,
pointless in your palm like lost teeth.

Someone in the university who knew
anatomy could tell you its incisors
are full-grown, ground down. Sign

of an elderly specimen too slow
to escape wings muffled by the night.

Sufficient witness. This disassembled skeleton
of the old skunk freshly plucked
of fur and flesh is proof enough

Owl will eat anything.

CONCERT CANCELLED
BY COLD SPELL

They hobble from the fishpond every fall
before the freeze, to congregate on logs,
quaking as their leader clears his throat.
Nimble toes tremble: Frog feet cling
to twigs (their very soles are chilled and wet).
Each throat throbs with a performer's pride—
They know a crowd will flock to hear their song.

Picture people perched on stones or tall
stumps, eager to applaud! The truth is frogs
in the fall won't sing at all, not a blessed note.
Our hearts remain mute until the spring
loosens our lungs. Likewise frogs forget
they cannot sing, although they've often tried
and failed. They *think* they can, but they're wrong.

WAITING FOR WINTER

1

I think of my name, Julia Grahm,
and hold my hands so in a circle,
making my mind obey my mind.
Alone in a harsh room in some home,
no sound but my breathing for hours.
Light cleanses the floor of its color.
On the walls no mirrors, no chairs
in the corners or tables or flowers.

My flesh has forsaken its shadow.
My eyes wander to one window
which offers a view of the orchard,
apples and pears long since picked
and packed. Leaves purple the grass.
Rubbed to its sheen like a pewter plate,
behind bare branches sleeps the lake.

In all that ache of autumn
the only woman—Why must I wait
for the weather to turn? And turn again?
Caught up in a crowd of acquaintances
I want to feel the wishes of my flesh
though I know that I'm dreaming—
No one is here, no one is coming.

2

It's impossible to move one muscle
even to music, unless you love.
Look at me, I want to see
the swift sex of birds!
Spring sun melting the mud!
To be born in a warm season like the bulbs—
The first sound of sin that you hear in your skin.

However, it's almost the end
of November and over blue fields
flakes are sown or scattered without care.
A pocket of snow collects in the crotch
of every available tree,
and I'm frozen in my fortieth year
of this dream, waiting for winter.

I keep my wits. I say I'm a wise woman.
Then an ice storm strikes so deep
it chokes the spring in the lake for weeks
and won't warm. Well water sleeps.
The orchard claws at the wind.
My bones are blind but they believe
what they are told of cold despair.
Now it is coming, now it is here.

WHEN WE WAKE UP

When we wake up it is winter—

the purity of the pale clouds
the semen color of the clouds

this color is everywhere
look

when we wake up
the same shade once more—

the secret shining in the ice
the skin of light over the lake.

OWL HAS CLOSED HIS EYES

Owl has closed his eyes to the cold spell.
He will not be a witness to winter,
it appears to displease him. Moreover
he won't complain, he voices no comment
(though his toes are freezing).
Back toes braced, tense talons
biting a bare limb, Owl
could not sit more stiff or still
if he were stuffed and mounted.

Never mind that a north wind
arrived without warning
to spin the feathered weathervane
on each henhouse, catching the cocks
quite by surprise—those who woke
Rock Lake this morning with their icy cries.
Their ruling vanity ruffled, if not routed.
An amusing prank, you think?

Owl cares nothing about it.

FATHER TEIN AT FIVE O'CLOCK

"from the heart's abundance
the mouth speaks"
— *St. Matthew*

December 10. Slight comfort in my speech
but winter settles hard. Our worst sins no
longer terrify, their names recall accounts
of an old plague. Its fever wanes in each.
In all my rhetoric there's not one ounce
of shame, the women are convinced I'm callow.

My soul remains mute when I pursue
meditation, hiking through the raw snow.
"At times," they say, "aloof, as if his lot
were his alone." At times, I believe the Jew
suffers more. Perhaps. Although I've not
heard his psalms sung well, outside Chicago.

I have been asked to dine tonight on diced
carrots, meatloaf, biscuits. Must I go?
(You need not press your servant; by half-past
I shall be reading Nones.) Briefly, my Christ,
listen: on the walk many steps are fast
and late. Ah, were the hour only so.

AT JULIA'S HOUSE

Carollers leave the drifting road. To reach
Julia's house they weave like mourners in a row

crossing the burial ground beyond her barn.
For miles around the rising tide of snow

floods the farms... When the boys halt, the girls
lean in their woolen arms. Their candles quake and glow.

They wait, whispering steam. Like lantern lights
they shadow and gleam until they sway

her mind. Still she perches in the rose
window-seat to learn if they will stay.

Now her only choice is to listen for their singing,
she cannot hear their voices, and why do they delay?

IT IS THE DEAD OF WINTER

It is the dead of winter when the damp wings
of ashes waft past window panes
then settle onto sills above the street.
And whether you lie dozing in a drifted sheet
or sit upright twining your hair
into a yellow halo,
you are not here...

O, open your eyes,
otherwise you are
gone now.

      Not here.

Where?
Where is your mind?
Give me your hand.

      Do you know me? When did we meet?

Love, do you know
it is the dead of winter and the damp wings
of snowflakes press like lace
against the glass. Now they blow loose

and dance in the flood
of a lamp, falling and falling
into black traffic.

Show me that,
she said, then hid
her hand behind her head.

Give me your hand.
See the hill of snow growing on the window.

Where did you go today in the snow?

O, nowhere.

Nowhere or here
it's the same, all day seems to mean...

The snow is rising on the pane.
I see a pure hill. A peak.
It's so white now
I can't tell where the light is in the street.

Where will you go after dark in the snow?

Home. I don't know.

Please do not be bothered about me.
I have money, we are not poor people.

What do you want with your wallet?
Let me see, what's in it?
Show me your wife.

No, no.

    Please show me
    her picture.
    Is she pretty?

You must rest.
It's time I left.

    O, be good. You said you would—
    Say something odd to make me laugh.

Can I leave
you like this?

    You'll be back, I know you will.

Be still, be still,
Love of my life.

EARTH GIVES

Earth gives a single groan,
that sound of the pond in winter when the black flint
of goodbye is frozen in it.

The only owl to notice this noise
flops from her branch and begins to hunt
the white meadow. Tomorrow.

BLIZZARD

February 14. The first day. Not one valentine
delivered. "Unnatural," sighed
her green-eyed cousin from St. Louis.
Every street had sunk from view.
Across the county a white wind blew
the prairie flat as any fire.
Sleet rattled the bare bushes.
"Bushes? Where?"
"Our lilac, dear.
Remember that hedge behind the porch?"

Every lawnchair tumbled into the pasture.
Saturday night the snow sat down
under the wind, wet as paint; discouraged
her search for furniture. Without fail
Sunday the two would trudge to church.
The wind with something else in mind
locked her door. Sealed it shut
halfway up. They brewed a pot of mint
tea; took to rummaging her cupboard.
That night they drank a deep sleep.

What hour was it called them forth
in a voice clear as ice? All day
the grey cloth scrubbed her kitchen

window. Light without heat. Each breath
a silver blossom nodding on no stem.
A pervading chill in which their fingers
closed around two saucers
as if asking grace. Until time
once more to sip her aromatic tea
and whiskey in a cheerful crystal cup.

"Will it snow and snow all year?"

"Perhaps."

"How do you endure?"

"Sit, dear. Let me pour."

THE CHILDREN WHO LEFT

After school we stood in the snow
beyond the railbed black with soot
O world of softly falling flame
so cold we cried while we attacked
the thundering train. On window panes
our snowballs blossomed, powerless
as prairie flowers. Each crowded car
roared toward twilight unperturbed.
Mothers and clerks and raw reserve
troops in leather jackets. Older
men muffled in overcoats
against the greasy weather of the smoker.

Always the brakeman understood
our shadow hope, swinging his lamp
cheerfully over the quick silver
rails shimmering toward Chicago.
Years ago. So young the chill
air stung our teeth. Air like ice
cracking. The chill children hear
in their parents' voices growing numb
while winter drifts above, below.
O world of softly falling time
that turns to flame! Our feet on fire,
our boots stamped and stamped the burning snow.

While winter drifts above, below,
who lit that blaze beneath the sky?
Beyond the buried miles, that far
horizon gleams and flickers; bleak
clouds unfold like factory smoke—
Blame the brakeman, waving his glad
lantern, lifting his little flask
before us. Before our eyes fled
aboard a dark car trailing flares
over the white fields, into the city
where you see us now. Distant
lights guttering under the dusk.

SPRING SNOW

Only you will keep me company. In all
our parish only you will listen
and resist reproach. Yet you must
shiver in this white shower
of spring snow. We turn to watch
our footprints melting to monstrous size.
Frail flakes like stars light in your hair.
They dampen, die out, as we walk
above the frozen creek and still
you will not ask. The question
pulses in your wrist: Why
did I try to take my life? That rumor

you heard was true. I sliced a vein
with that horn-handled hunting knife
Simon Skoronsky left me on the night
he drove east to study philosophy.
My only friend of my own sex. This
I confess. Affections among men
allow few words. Now I speak
only to you, my tongue tied
in a knot of envy. One day our scholar
Skoronsky will lecture in a university.
I miss the play of his mind and mine
in unfenced fields of thought. Only doubt

delivers us from error, just as rain
provokes the spring to green. Out
of Holy Name Hospital my desire
for you has healed my heart. Stung
to life by your young touch. But look
how Rock Creek lies white as a corpse.
Some lost soul left unburied,
his long legs under the trees. Yes:
This is my body. Christ! My flesh
is pale as the aging April snow.
After forty a priest
feels ice in his throat. My blood runs cold.

How many souls do I set on fire
with love of the only God
they might ever know? Do any learn
to love because I give
my simple example? No, they shun me
unless I say their dead cannot die.
Unless I say they will live forever, and lie
at peace in a land lovelier than this. Instead,
I do for them what the devil does
for me. I help them to see
the fallacy of their perfection
mirrored in myself... More, I cannot do.

Months ago on a walk like this we heard
the first wolf of winter howl
her thirst, or hunger. Was her cry

yours and mine? One howl
in the throat of night
for the hunger in us all?
O love, I believe the answer
to that question is that question:
Nature is not what we thought—
We know what we want to know.

I want to walk no further but be warm
so I take your arm in mine
as we turn toward town and dusk
rushes to meet us in the hissing snow.

TO BRING SPRING

Free of their scarves, their woolen coats,
   girls toss their hair
      in the gun-blue dusk,
         dancing on
the porch. Their laughter spills
   across the lawn; a breeze tails
      off Rock Lake cold
         with the steel smell
of rainwater. Frail
   lanterns in the paper evening air
      blow half-way dark
         and half-way back.

Late in the morning a dead season lies
   hardly glimmering
      on the hill
         or leans at the porch in the sun.
Robins bob among the mud and green
   shoots sprouting in the pasture.
      The white colt, his winter legs
         slack, strolls
up from his hay, deliberately
   he trudges the sodden hill. Down
      and up the rise
         apple branches blossom.

A slow girl, her black hair braided,
   and two tall sisters strip
      the lanterns off. The sisters
        with a certain arch,
like divers, loft
   the lamp shells down
      to their friend. All three walk out
        the drive where sunlight blows
under the eaves. The last girl
   cradling several globes
      in her bare arms
        yellow and blue and rose.

THE FOURTH DAY OF THE FLOOD

1

Upriver the wreckage of the railway trestle
twists in the current.
Its steel girders have gone under,
the vertical beams bend like green willows
into the water.
                    Two tow-trucks, half-submerged,
loll on their backs: giant beetles unable
to right themselves.
                    Elms uprooted, tumble
down the torrent. Roofs of coops collapse,
chickens drift in the river's rubble. Power
lines snap, spark. Downed poles criss-cross
the county. At dawn the town lies dark.

A thin light seeps through the rain.

The water whitens when the lightning flashes.

2

Nine pine coffins in the Grange Hall wait
for a common wake.
Six of pine a cedar crowd the nave
of St. Paul's.
                    In a shifting line we pack
sandbags against the sliding banks
of Rock River.
                    No sign of the man
who tried to raft to safety with his dog
and gun.
                    Then the lean dog thrashes
the water, washed along, leashed to one leg
of a shattered table.
                    Two women in waders
with a long-handled hoe hook the wood
to shore. And the shivering dog. Mueller the coroner
knows this sleek retriever, he's hunted with her owner.

3

Long deaf at seventy Julia Grahm still hears
thunder in her hands. Shuddering, she brews
an urn of coffee. Each crew pauses—
A young priest in a poncho fills our cups.

Thunder urges the line back to work—
Khaki sacks slump into place.

4

No crew can save the crumbling levee or the orchard road:
Fish swim through the leaves.
Like birds they glide among the limbs of the plum trees.
Families pace the hillside. They stop. Stare down
at us. Stare down at the islands
of their high old houses. Dogs whine
from the rooftops. They whine in the wind and rain.

A red stop sign peers across the flood.
In the wind we watch rowboats
bump about in the road—
The dogs bark at the boats.

5

Pain stops all speech: Each private ache
eats away at the spine, shoulder, knee.
Not one voice jokes, curses, sings, along the lunging line.
While the wind rages
we lift the sodden sand, sofa cushions, old mattresses.
Trucks groan to deliver their gravel.

6

Where the bank has broken the river spills
into a pool. We stop the flow, drain it off,
and discover the fox cub drowned in mud.
The weasel pinned in the arm of a pine.

Groundhogs, rabbits, cats, so many
small creatures innocent and unlucky—
Quiet in death as the wide-eyed cattle
found in the fields when the waters settle.

7

Through the din of the storm the line stoops
into evening. It stoops and slogs.
It bends, weaves, shoulders sagging,
hips and numb legs nudging,
boots sunk into the muck.
Hands touch raw hands.
Eyes meet and close. The line lifts
again: an act of love which gives
the hour a tenderness as real
as the ache that climbs each spine.
This grace that outlasts hope, this pain—
It holds us to our work, we hardly feel
the gale fall away.
                    The roaring dies
as the current lags. Our lame dance
halts. At rest we turn
downriver where the wind has run,
and all our faces share the rain.

A BALLAD FOR THE BRIDE

Under green elms green shallows spill,
the prairie blooms beneath its pack
of lean wolves. Weasels bleed their kill,
then run before the hunting hawk—

Merchants, farm hands, the younger cousin
come to visit, they learn in town
how Julia with strict devotion
has shed her dress and laid her down

on clear water, in cool shade.
There, last night, she saw, exact
as pain, the moon climb down to wade
Rock River. Now the ancient black

hearse, prodigious, has dignified
our brief procession: Coroner and priest
and the formal families all ride
slowly to her wedding feast—

The old hawk hovers near the river,
weasels rattle through the barns,
Julia has found her lover.
waiting with cold and open arms.

HOW HER SPIRIT RISES & RETURNS

1

Unlocked from the loom of the land, birds soar
        toward evening. They loop back
through the orchard, shuttling, shrill
        yellow in the boughs
in blossom, weaving songs, while her soul hastens
to leave the achievements of grass, water, trees.
        Acres in flower fall into dusk,
the blue burn of Rock Lake dims, intense,
        into its final flare like a spark of oil.
In solitude she finds our streets are lighted still
        by the eyes of every child,
every man or woman memory can conceive,
        silent as those stones, huge, angular, smoothed
only by harsh weather, which secure the shore.
        Or these, blunt-edged, abrupt,
hauled up by crane to compact the crumbling road
        into town, where we're not what we thought
        to become. Spirit released, unrealized,
Julia Grahm is no more the angel of our anxiety,
        the image of each hour woven in the wind
as all our hours are gathered stone by stone
into the black rain that fills the lake to its brim.

2

Beyond the burial ground her home no longer
dominates the dark. Night invites starlight.
Day by broken day welcomes the wind.
West windows open wide, curtains curling
in turbulent waves—in each trough the opulence
of apple, cherry, plum, the rife scents of every
spring that we store in the hive of memory.

3

Seventy years she was caring, crazed, loved, left
alone. At dawn her soul, revenant, seeking more
        vivid harmonies, she listens for the tongues
of leaves to lead her, incautious as the sun
        walking the water to the shore,
climbing the rocks, approaching the trees—
Morning among damp limbs, shadows of leaves,
        a girl dances across the grass
of seventy years. Each whirl unfolds her hair,
        she becomes the whistling voice we hear
beneath the wind. In the brush, in warming light.
        Its song, pervasive, swells. Green veins
throb. Once more the orchard is stirred by these
        melodies the woodthrush weaves.

EPILOGUE

THESE SMALL SONGS

Suppose we are unaware of time passing.
And all our hours are expended passing
into time. Let it seem so. Soon,
it's summer. This green evening
strung with cicada song.

                              A boat droning

across our violet sleep.

                         Let it

seem to. We'll wake and walk
into a warmer morning. We are
passing into time. If only
on the stony shore where we are.

Where pines hold one pose
hour by hour
against an unblinking glare,

their rare restraint
visible since noon
in that reflective light in which they lean

toward dusk
when a blue sun floats over

Rock Lake and
noiseless they

dive.
       Splash—

less shadows lengthen,
swimming far from shore.

Swimming their darkness over the water
not like a leaky net drawn
by a droning boat. More like night
itself, which catches and holds

the soul's attention. Utterly still

but for the boat. And these small songs
the cicadas sing, constant as clocks
that tell of something passing. Let it.

Carol Gardner

GEORGE KEITHLEY

George Keithley's poems have appeared in numerous collections, anthologies, and magazines. Author of the Book-of-the-Month Club *The Donner Party*, Mr. Keithley writes full-time and lives in Chico, California.